VIKING
TWITTER MARKETING

Chapter 1:

Getting Started with Twitter

Why Use Twitter?

Twitter is, without question, one of the most active, popular social platforms on the web. The platform has about 310 million monthly active users and an additional 550 million monthly viewers who don't login to their own accounts but merely consume other people's Tweets. About one-third of all US social media users are on Twitter and 80% of active users access the site via mobile. Somewhere around 500 million Tweets are sent per day which adds up to about 6,000 Tweets per second.

Businesses haven't missed out on the utility of Twitter. About 65% of US companies having 100+ employees are marketing on Twitter. There's good reason for this: The average Twitter user follows 5 businesses. 80% of Twitter users have mentioned a brand in their Tweets, 77% feel more positive about a brand when their Tweet is replied to by a business and 54% have taken some kind of action (e.g. purchase, sign up, visit site) after seeing a brand mentioned in a Tweet. So clearly this is a powerful platform for any business. Question is, how can you leverage it?

Developing Your Twitter Plan

Your Twitter plan should be in place before you even setup your Twitter account so you can start implementing and sticking with it from day one. If you attack Twitter half-heartedly and without a plan, you'll do what too many entrepreneurs do: you'll eventually let your Twitter marketing peter out. Nobody wants to look like that embarrassing business whose last Tweet was from 3 years ago (and there's a ton of those).

So generally, you want to put down a plan in writing that covers your day-to-day activity on Twitter. For example, maybe you'll send out 2 tweets per day, Monday through Saturday. Maybe you or one of your team members will do these tweets manually each day. Otherwise, perhaps your weekly plan will include one hour every Sunday where you draft and schedule each of your tweets for the coming week using a social media scheduling tool like Warlord Social Suite (sort of an Internet Marketing-friendly version of HootSuite). Then, maybe you plan on participating in Twitter Chats once each week to grow your following and network. Finally, your plan should include at least a daily check-in (preferably more than once per day) in which you check for questions, mentions, retweets, etc (and reply to them accordingly).

Setting Up Your Twitter Account

Setting up your brand's Twitter account seems simple enough, but here are some important guidelines. Your Twitter name should be your actual name or business name, while your handle should either be your business name or something catchy that represents your business. Keep in mind, the handle is the "nickname" that you see after the "@" sign and it has a character limit, so your full name or business name might not fit as your handle in its entirety.

Next, you'll want to setup a powerful bio. Your bio should do two things: Accurately represent and introduce people to your brand and also be optimized for search results. You're limited to 160 characters (at the time of this writing) in your bio so you'll need to choose carefully what you squeeze in there. Some important considerations for your bio are hashtags you want people to find you with, a brand or business description, your mission or purpose (on Twitter, specifically), and maybe your job/position in your company if you've got a personal profile.

After that, you'll want to choose a profile URL. Most businesses tend to simply put their homepage here. That's okay, but you should actually be aiming for something more special. Instead of your general homepage, try creating a landing page specifically for Twitter users who come to your site via your profile URL. This way they can see something relevant and maybe you can collect leads (and track how many of your leads come from twitter!) or sales or showcase a Twitter follower-specific offer of some sort.

Finally, you'll want to iron out the visual representation of your brand by choosing a profile pic, a cover image, and a color scheme. Your profile pic could be your own portrait (make it snazzy and professional) or your business logo. Your cover image should be catchy and fit well with the rest of your brand image. Consider throwing a call-to-action (CTA) in there too. As for your colors, just make sure they match your brand and convey the feeling you want your followers to experience. The general idea with all of these things is to keep your brand representation consistent across all your social media platforms.

Chapter 2:

Commencing Your Twitter Operations

The next step is to introduce yourself on twitter with an initial tweet. Ideally, this should not be salesy. Opt instead for something catchy, funny, and/or helpful and consider using an image relevant to your brand for that first Tweet. Remember, this will be the first time people have seen your brand on Twitter. You don't want it to look like an annoying advertisement. Make that first impression a positive one.

Start Implementing Your Plan

Once you've done that, it's time to start implementing your Twitter plan. Start drafting those daily Tweets and keep in mind this is about consistent social media exposure over time. Don't expect to become the biggest viral sensation on the web overnight and don't be disappointed if/when you don't get much in the way of results in the very beginning. That will come later, but you have to stick to your plan!

Here are some guidelines for your daily and weekly Twitter activities. Find a balance between promotional stuff and useful stuff, and lean more towards the latter. Throw a bit of funny/entertaining into the mix from time to time as well. If you're out of ideas, don't hesitate to curate/share content from other entities like blog posts or articles, and always mention the source using the "@" sign. That @ will notify the source of your post and can be a good way to foster goodwill and relationships.

Another guideline is to include hashtags in most of your tweets. Make sure these are relevant and try not to throw in more than two or three in one tweet. Statistics show that if you include more than that you risk annoying people and losing engagement. Also, be generous with retweets. Retweets are great because they are an easy way to fill your weekly tweet quota and can also foster goodwill and relationships with other Twitter users. Be sure to include a comment explaining why you're retweeting or what your thoughts are.

Chapter 3:
Expanding Your Following

If you follow the guidelines in the previous chapter, then after a few days you should have at least a handful of followers. Now it's time to crank things up a notch. Let's go over some methods for building your following even more.

First, follow relevant members of your market and you'll often get followed in return. Next, try to interact in real time throughout the day. This will become apparent to Twitter users and you'll appear as alert, responsive, and engaged. Pay close attention to trending hashtags and topics so you can leverage their momentum. Ensure you mention/cite people in Tweets using the "@" sign. Many will return the favor.

What you tweet matters too. In addition to textual tweets or mentions of interesting articles, be sure to include some catchy media. Use relevant, attractive images. Include videos from time to time. Make it a point to proactively encourage engagement with questions and polls. This provokes responses and gives would-be followers the impression that you're there to listen, not just to talk. And yes, those cheesy quote images work too. All of these practices will increase engagement, sharing, and so on.

In addition to these methods, it's important to follow some basic Twitter etiquette and maintain the following you have. Although scheduling tools like Warlord Social Suite are great for the majority of your activity, you should also make time for a bit of responsive, manual, real-time interaction during the week. People can tell when you're using your Twitter account as an automated advertising machine and they'll unfollow you in a heartbeat. On a related note: Don't **ever** purchase followers. You'll see others doing it and you'll likely be tempted. But most of these followers will be bots and you WILL destroy your brand and reputation.

Chapter 4:
Achieving ROI

So you've put a ton of time, work, and perhaps money into your Twitter operations. Now it's time to capitalize on it. Remember this is not a one time thing, so don't suddenly ruin all the work you've done by abruptly trying to sell stuff to all of your followers. It won't work and you'll have wasted everything. Instead, make this the new normal. Stick to the plan. Keep building your audience. Gradually and gently start seeking a return on this investment.

Remember what we said about balance? Useful and entertaining should be the norm, while salesy stuff should be the exception. It's time to start thinking about the exception. Although Twitter can certainly bring in sales, it's best to just periodically use it to build your list and familiarize people with your content and off-Twitter presence. Post tweets that link to a landing page designed to generate leads. Invite people to read your blog posts or articles or to watch your videos. If you insist on selling things from time to time, just try to keep it to a minimum and maybe limit it to special deals or exciting new products.

Battle Plan

This guide has been pretty exhaustive, but it doesn't mean a thing unless you act on it and remain consistent. To that end, here's a quick battle plan that should get you on your way to Twitter marketing success:

Step 1: Develop your marketing plan.

Step 2: Set up your account to match your branding.

Step 3: Start implementing your plan with daily tweets.

Step 4: Diversify your Tweeting style and content to maximize engagement and follower-building.

Step 5: Gently and subtly start achieving ROI by promoting your off-Twitter content, free offers, and special deals.

Don't wait. Start taking action today!

www.ingramcontent.com/pod-product-compliance
Lightning Source LLC
Chambersburg PA
CBRC090852210326
41597CB00011B/177